A GIFT FOR

_____

FROM

_____

Dr. Henry Cloud
& Dr. John Townsend

What to Do When You Don't Know What to Do

Discouragement & Depression

God Will Make a Way

INTEGRITY®
PUBLISHERS

WHAT TO DO WHEN YOU DON'T KNOW WHAT TO DO:
DISCOURAGEMENT & DEPRESSION

Copyright © 2005 by Henry Cloud and John Townsend.

Published by Integrity Publishers, a division of Integrity Media, Inc., 5250 Virginia Way, Suite 110, Brentwood, TN 37027.

HELPING PEOPLE WORLDWIDE EXPERIENCE *the* MANIFEST PRESENCE *of* GOD.

Published in association with Yates & Yates, LLP, Literary Agents, Orange, California.

Unless otherwise indicated, Scripture quotations are taken from The Holy Bible, New International Version (NIV), copyright ©1973, 1978, 1984, International Bible Society. Used by permission of Zondervan Bible Publishers.

Other Scripture quotations are taken from the following sources:

New American Standard Bible (NASB), © 1960, 1977, 1995 by the Lockman Foundation.

The Holy Bible, New Living Translation (NLT), copyright ©1996. Used by permission of Tyndale House Publishers, Inc., Wheaton, Illinois. All rights reserved.

Cover and interior design: UDG | DesignWorks, www.udgdesignworks.com

ISBN 1-59145-350-X

Printed in the United States of America

05 06 07 08 09   LBM   9 8 7 6 5 4 3 2 1

Contents

Prologue

Eric, a successful, married businessman in his late forties, came to see me (John) about a problem with depression. No matter what he did, he felt very down all the time—discouraged, hopeless, and with a lack of enjoyment in anything he did. It didn't make sense to him, for his life, while not perfect, was reasonably OK.

Eric was at that stage of life in which things should have been getting smoother for him. His wife, Laura, and he were happily married. Their two children were in college, and the "high maintenance" years of parenting were behind them.

His place in his company as a senior vice president of a home-building group was secure, and a good fit for him. So as far as life struggles went, there wasn't a lot to go on.

I asked Eric, "At this point, what have you done so far to deal with the depression?" He said, "Well, I have been praying a lot for God to help me and reading my Bible. And, since the kids are gone, I have more free time, so I volunteer at the church and I've started playing golf. Thought that would give me a lift. But nothing really helps. I still feel like I'm swimming in mud most of the time. It's just awful."

I empathized with Eric. If you've never experienced true depression, you wouldn't wish it on your worst enemy. It is a darkness inside of you that you cannot get away from or talk yourself out of.

"What about your relationships?" I asked.

"You mean friends? I have a good group of guys that I play golf with."

"How do they handle your depression?"

"Well," Eric replied, "that's not the sort of thing we really talk about. I think that's a pretty personal subject. Besides, they would think I'm nuts, being depressed with the kind of life I've got."

I asked, "So who knows how you feel?"

Eric thought a minute. "Well, Laura does, but she feels pretty helpless about it. She doesn't know what to do, so she tries to help me see the positive things in life and stay active. And God knows my insides, of course. He's the one I want to heal me."

"What if I told you," I asked, "that you need more than just God in that place?"

"I'd say that you were telling me that God isn't enough for me—and I have a problem with that."

"Well, I agree with you there," I said. "I do believe that God is enough to meet all our needs and solve all our struggles. However, the Bible teaches that God has designed us to not only open up to him and his love and grace but also to people who will be kind and safe with us."

Eric was a little confused. "I guess that still sounds like trusting man, not God."

So, to illustrate my point, I took Eric through several verses from the Bible, such as:

> . . . it is not good for the man to be alone. (Genesis 2:18, NIV)

> Two are better than one, because they have a good return for their work: If one falls down, his friend can help him up. But pity the man who falls and has no one to help him up! (Ecclesiastes 4:9–12, NIV)

> . . . we can comfort those in any trouble with the comfort we ourselves have received from God. (2 Corinthians 1:4, NIV)

I explained, "We all have a need for the grace of God, and also for the grace that he provides through other people. Without it, we don't have access to the understanding, kindness, and support that he designed us to experience. And my hunch is that you are sort of out of gas, relationally speaking, since you didn't think it was OK to let others in. And that is a leading cause of depression."

Eric started putting the pieces together. "You know," he said, "the family I grew up in was a very loving one. My parents really cared. But at the same time, if I was afraid or lonely, it wasn't really OK to talk about that. They would just shrug those problems off and tell me to think better thoughts and stay busy."

"Sounds like life today," I said.

"It's a lot like today," Eric agreed. "I have always enjoyed my marriage and kids, and my friends and my work. But I never thought I should talk to anyone about my problems."

"Right," I agreed. "And it may be that now that the kids are gone and life has slowed a little, with less work stress, your circumstances have allowed your own relational isolation and emptiness to come out. That may be why this has happened at this juncture for you."

It made sense to Eric, and he got to work. He started concentrating on his fears of letting others in. He joined a small home group at church that was into relationships. He began working on trusting others and letting them know him. It took some time, as he was used to talking to others about their lives but avoiding his own. But gradually, as he became connected on deeper levels to a few safe people, Eric began realizing his depression was resolving. He felt more energy, more hopefulness, and more life inside himself.

Eric's depression had served as a signal to him that he was very alone inside. Some depressions are signals for other issues, but this was his. And so, when he became grounded with people who cared and wanted to know his "insides," the signal was no longer needed, and the depression went away.

Depression, though painful, is quite a common condition. If you suffer from it, you are far from alone. And the good news is that when you don't know what to do about depression, there are effective and helpful answers and solutions—and a lot of sound hope—for your depression. Read on and find out.

PART I:
EIGHT PRINCIPLES TO GUIDE YOU OUT OF DEPRESSION

Most people cannot see God's way out of depression and discouragement because the darkness they experience makes them wonder if there really is a way at all. Or if there is, they don't know how to find it. Their depression is so deep and overwhelming that it has left them feeling hopeless.

Well, there is good news. There is a way, and you can find it when you activate your faith in God by following eight principles in this section. We will have more to say specifically about overcoming depression in the section that follows this one. Think of these principles as foundation stones. You must lay them in your life so that you can build on them the structures you need to win over your problem.

Meaningful faith must be placed

in a real Person

who knows

the way for you and

promises to lead you on it.

That's God.

Begin Your Journey with God

When we speak of God, we don't mean some kind of vague, universal force; we mean a real person, complete with mind, will, and the power to act in our lives. So when we say that faith and trust will carry you to victory over your depression, we're not talking about warm religious feelings or an exercise in positive thinking. Meaningful faith must be placed in a real Person who knows the way for you and promises to lead you on it. That's God. So our first principle for healing your depression is to *begin your journey with God.* You can't do it without him.

Your need for God's help is no more a weakness than your need for air. We did not create ourselves, nor were we designed to create our own way in life. God wired us to depend on him. When you exercise faith in him, you position yourself to accomplish superhuman feats, which is what overcoming depression may require. You are reaching beyond human strength and knowledge and tapping into God's infinite strength and knowledge.

Most of us, when we don't know what to do in the face of a difficult or painful situation, do one of two things. First, we repeat what didn't work before, but this time we try harder. Chronic dieters, for example, try to muster up just a little more will power, and "this time it will work." Second, we stop trying altogether. *I will never stop overeating, so what's the use?* The first reaction often spawns the second. Trying to get through life on your own limited strength and knowledge leads to futility and loss of hope.

But in God's economy, getting to the end of yourself is the beginning of hope. Jesus said, "God blesses those who realize their need for him" (Matthew 5:3 NLT). When you admit your helplessness and ask God for help, you transcend your own limitations and God's resources become available to you.

God's resources cannot be earned; they can only be received as a gift when we, in humility, acknowledge our need for our Creator. He's ready to get involved in your life. All you have to do is say yes to him. Then he will provide what you need to overcome even the most debilitating depression.

Sometimes his way will be truly miraculous, and sometimes it will involve a lot of work and change on your part. Often it won't be the way you thought you needed. But when God makes a way, it works.

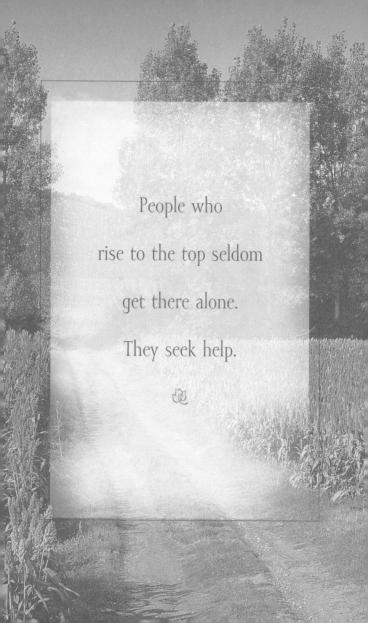

People who

rise to the top seldom

get there alone.

They seek help.

Choose Your Traveling Companions Wisely

When I (Henry) was a youngster, Jack Nicklaus was king of golf, and as an aspiring golfer, I thought he was almost a god. Then I heard that he consulted a golf pro for help on his swing. I was stunned. Teachers were for people who didn't know what they were doing. I have learned a lot since then. People who rise to the top seldom get there alone. They seek help.

This story illustrates our second principle of God's way of overcoming depression: *Surround*

> One of the ways God works is through other people.

yourself with people who are committed to support you, encourage you, assist you, and pray for you.

One of the ways God works is through other people. Solomon said, "Two are better than one . . . If one falls down, his friend can help him up. But pity the man who falls and has no one to help him up!" (Ecclesiastes 4:9–10). Some of these people will just show up in your life, sent at just the right time. Others you have to seek out. They can range from professionals to a neighbor or friend at church. Here are some important qualities to look for as you select your support team.

SUPPORT. In overcoming depression, you are pushing uphill. Depression can drain you of emotional, physical, and spiritual strength. You need the kind of person who will show up at your door anytime to help you.

LOVE. You need the safety net of people who love you deeply just as you are, even when you don't feel lovable.

COURAGE. You will encounter risk and fear. When the task looks too daunting to face, your support team will build your courage.

FEEDBACK. You can't see yourself objectively. You need honest people who are not afraid to correct you when you are wrong.

WISDOM. You don't have all the wisdom and knowledge you need to make it. Look for wise people through whom God will speak to you.

EXPERIENCE. Seek out the experience of others who have been through depression and know what you are going through.

MODELING. It is difficult to do what we have never seen done. Seek out and learn from those who have recovered from depression.

VALUES. Your value system will guide you as you turn your life around. We learn values from others, and others support us by enforcing values. Stay close to people who share your values; stay away from those who don't.

ACCOUNTABILITY. You need people who will monitor your progress and keep you on track. Look for people who will ask the tough questions: Where are you failing? What kind of help do you need?

You may already have in your life people who meet your need for support. If so, explain that you need them on your journey to recovery. Ask if they will be available to provide accountability, feedback, or support. They will probably feel honored and valued that you would ask.

If you run short of supportive friends, consider joining a structured support system, such as a Bible study group. Share with these people your struggle and ask for their prayers and input. You will reap great benefits when you allow a loving support group to help you on your journey.

3

Place High Value on Wisdom

O ften we feel hopeless and don't know where to turn because we lack vital information about depression and its cure. A key way out of despair is to find these missing pieces of wisdom and apply them to our problem. God tells us that wisdom produces hope: "Know also that wisdom is sweet to your soul; if you find it, there is a future hope for you, and your hope will not be cut off" (Proverbs 24:14).

So our third principle for finding God's way out of depression is this: *Recognize the value and need for the missing pieces of wisdom in your life; then ask God to show them to you.*

WISDOM COMES FROM GOD. James tells us to ask God for the wisdom we need: "If any of you lacks wisdom, he should ask God, who gives generously to all without finding fault . . ." (James 1:5). God knows what to do even when you don't. Ask him for answers and he will provide them.

GOD USES OTHERS. You may not know what to do in your situation, but there is somebody out there who does. Find that someone. Whenever I (Henry) am dealing with a difficult financial situation, I call a certain friend who has great wisdom in that area, and I lean on him for good advice. I have other people I call for other needs.

When facing depression, you are wise to seek out people who have knowledge, expertise, and experience in that area—people who have been there, done that, and gotten through it. Keep asking around until you find them.

Seek structured wisdom. Usually dealing with depression requires more than good advice from friends or others. You also need structured and professional sources of wisdom. And there are a great number of services out there, including trained counselors, support groups, and psychiatrists. You don't need to re-invent the wheel for your situation. There is help available, already in place.

Don't use cost as an excuse not to take advantage of professional help. Yes, some treatments are expensive, but many are free, and financial assistance is often available from the government and other agencies. Ferret out all your possibilities.

Here is a sampling of places to start looking:

- Professionals in your area of need

- Self-help groups

- Pastors

- Churches

- Community colleges

- Seminars

- Books, tapes, and videos

- Workshops

- Retreats

One caution: Make sure the resources you uncover are authentic. Get referrals from people you trust—your friends, your support group, your doctor, or your pastor.

THE ORDER OF THINGS. God has put you in a universe of order. Things work because of the laws God set in place at creation. Part of the way for you to win over depression has already been made in how he created life to work. Your task is to find the wisdom that is already there. So search for his wisdom with all your strength and apply it wholeheartedly.

4

Leave Your Baggage Behind

W e all hate dragging a million pieces of luggage through a crowded airport. What if you had to tote a couple of suitcases, backpacks, and carry-on bags everywhere you went? It would weigh you down and hold you back. It's the same when overcoming depression. Emotional baggage can weigh you down and hold you back. Our fourth principle for finding God's way out of depression is to *leave your baggage behind.*

By baggage we mean bad stuff from the past.

We've all experienced difficult events and relationships, emotional hurts, divorces, serious mistakes, tragic accidents, or loss of a loved one. Ideally, these events are resolved as they happen. But often pain is stuffed instead of dealt with; offenders are not forgiven; fears are not confronted; conflicts are not resolved, leaving us with past feelings and patterns of behavior that impact the present. That's baggage. You can be sure that some of your baggage is directly related to your depression, and you can't be fully healed until you deal with it.

Here are five practical tips for helping you discard baggage.

1. AGREE THAT YOU HAVE A PAINFUL PAST. Acknowledge that painful things have happened to you that were not resolved. If you don't work through them, they will prevent your healing. So the first step is to confess to yourself and to God that you have these issues.

2. INCLUDE OTHERS IN YOUR HEALING AND GRIEVING. Seek from others the care and healing you need to resolve these issues. Pouring out your hurt to others who love you opens the door to comfort, encouragement, healing, and support. This openness is often difficult for people in depression, but start by doing what you can.

3. RECEIVE FORGIVENESS. Getting rid of baggage means being free of the guilt and shame of past failures and sins. God will forgive you for anything you have ever done, no matter how bad. The Bible promises, "For as high as the heavens are above the earth, so great is his love for those who fear him; as far as the east is from the west, so far has he removed our transgressions from us" (Psalm 103:11–12).

Your past failures and mistakes may also have alienated you from certain people. You must go to them, humbly confess your wrong, and receive forgiveness. Once you know you are forgiven,

> You still carry pain, anger, and perhaps hatred. You must forgive these people.

accepted, and loved, you can then re-enter life and begin moving on.

4. FORGIVE OTHERS. Some of your baggage may be hurts you received from others. You still carry pain, anger, and perhaps hatred. You must forgive these people. Take your cue from God, who has forgiven you. If you don't forgive, resentment will eat away at your heart. When you forgive another, you release that person from your right to exact punishment and retribution from them. And you release your own baggage of pain and resentment in the process.

5. SEE YOURSELF THROUGH NEW EYES. Another kind of baggage is the distorted view of ourselves we learned in past relationships or situations. We tend to see ourselves through the eyes of others who are important to us. And depending on whether that view is positive or negative,

we either feel valued or devalued. A realistic self-view will be balanced, recognizing strengths as well as weaknesses and growth areas.

Find this view by seeing yourself through God's eyes, for he loves you unconditionally and values you highly. Add to this the view you get from those who love you as God does. Let this *new you* replace the distorted picture that has caused you such grief.

Holding on to the baggage of the past will disable your search for victory over depression. Ask God to help you leave it behind.

In your life,

the buck stops with you.

When addressing any problem,

you need to step up

to the plate and take charge.

Own Your Faults and Weaknesses

I n your life, the buck stops with you. When addressing a problem like depression, you need to step up to the plate and take charge. It's your job to do what God gives you to do. And it's your job to accept the blame for the failures that are truly your own failures, not someone else's. Our fifth principle for God's way to recovery is that you *take responsibility for your life, own up to your faults, and accept blame where it is justified.*

The apostle Paul wrote, "Continue to work out your salvation with fear and trembling, for it

> Sometimes we have to take responsibility for situations that are not our fault.

is God who works in you to will and to act according to his good purpose" (Philippians 2:12–13). Now that God has saved you, it's your responsibility to live a life that reflects him. But notice that you are not alone in your efforts. God is there with you, empowering you. And this partnership between you and him accomplishes your goal.

Sometimes we have to take responsibility for situations that are not our fault. The man who is unfairly laid off must own up to the situation and start looking for another job. The abused wife must seek counseling.

Determining who is at fault isn't as important as determining who will do something about it. The latter "who" is you. Whoever is at fault, what matters is taking ownership to correct the problem. As you do, God will show you his way.

When we take ownership for what happens in our lives, we are empowered to make changes—to develop plans, tackle situations, and right wrongs. People who take charge of their lives are active people with real initiative. Ownership also frees us from false hopes, from discouragement and passivity, and to take risks and test-drive possible solutions.

When you take ownership and invite God to move in, he does it. He will get involved in moving you to success in overcoming your depression. Our role is to seek him, take charge of our own circumstances, and trust him to do for us what only he can do.

Welcome your problems as

gifts from God

to help you

become a better person.

6

Embrace Problems
as Gifts

S ome people hit a problem and stop dead in
their tracks—they feel stuck and hopeless.
All they want is to get rid of it as soon as possible. Other people find something useful in
problems. They ask, "What can I learn from this
experience? What does God want to change in
me?" This is our sixth principle for finding God's
way out of depression: *Welcome your problems as
gifts from God to help you become a better person.*

There's nothing wrong with trying to solve a
problem and alleviate the pain. But instead of
rushing to the most immediate fix, we must use

the problem to see our lives from God's perspective and find God's way through it.

And God's perspective is quite different. We might compare it to how differently a physician and a patient view pain. You come to the doctor in agony wanting a shot or a pill to make the pain go away. And you want it *now*. But your physician knows your pain is a sign of a deeper problem. He prescribes even more pain: surgery and physical therapy.

It's a choice all of us have to make at some point: You can demand immediate relief, knowing that your problem will recur. Or you can go through the healing process and resolve the problem once and for all. That's the choice you face when dealing with depression. God loves you, and like your physician, he is less concerned about your immediate comfort than about your long-term health.

The Bible tells us, "Consider it pure joy, my brothers, whenever you face trials of many kinds, because you know that the testing of your faith develops perseverance" (James 1:2–3). God's way is not *out* of your problem but *through* it. That's how we learn from our difficulties and find God's way.

When facing depression, you first need to look upward, toward God. He is like a storm raining down on a stagnant stream clogged with debris. As the torrent floods the stream, the debris is broken up and the flow resumes.

Second, you must look *inward*. Let God take you on a journey into yourself. He will shine a lantern of truth into the recesses of your heart, illuminating attitudes, wounds, hurts, weaknesses, and perspectives where you need to submit to his touch.

Problems are also a gift in that they help us *normalize* pain—to expect it as a regular part of life. We tend to think that bad things shouldn't happen to us, and we react in anger, denial, or despair when they do. But this doesn't alter the reality of the pain.

You must give up your protest about the unfairness of your problems and come to a place of acceptance. Only then can you learn what choices, paths, lessons, and opportunities are available to you. Accept pain as part of life. Accept that you don't have all the answers. Acceptance helps us to adapt to the way things really are, and to trust God.

Our problems help us identify with Jesus's sufferings. He loves us deeply, and our rebellion hurts him. But instead of finding a way out, he works through it. While he redeems, restores, and forgives us, he suffers. But he endures it because it's the only way. That is our model for dealing with pain. Identifying with his pain draws us closer to him, to see life as it really is and patiently take whatever steps are necessary to resolve the problem. Following the pattern of Jesus deepens and matures us.

Don't tolerate your depression, but don't ask God to just make the symptoms vanish instantly. Work through it God's way, and accept the gift of what you learn from the process.

7

Take Life as It Comes

I (John) have a bone disease called osteopenia. My bones are too porous, and they break easier than normal bones. I am on a special diet and a regimen of bone-strengthening exercises. I get an annual x-ray to check my progress. I would love to get more frequent progress reports, but bones change too slowly for that. The waiting is difficult, but it has taught me that I am not the master of time. I can't speed it up. I must let time have its way.

Our seventh principle for following God's way relates to what I am learning through my osteopenia: *We must allow time for God to work.*

Though I believe that God performs instantaneous miracles, it seems that his norm is a time-consuming process. Therefore, you must allow time for his process to happen.

Still, it's not easy to wait. When things don't happen quickly, we tend to become impatient, frustrated, and ready to give up. However, those who insist on shortcuts and quick fixes tend to repeat the same problems over and over, getting nowhere.

You've heard the saying "Time heals all wounds." Time heals nothing. It's futile to wait passively for God to change circumstances, for help to appear, or for your feelings to change. Such inaction will stick you in a holding pattern where you'll become discouraged when healing doesn't occur. You don't simply wait for a sprained knee to heal. You get a brace and do the physical therapy. Time is the context for our involvement in the process. When you invite God into your life and participate with him in the process, you will begin to see results. So do your part. Seek help and surround yourself with support and accountability. The more engaged you are, the less you will feel the pressure of time.

As nature has seasons, so do our lives. Solomon wrote, "There is a time for everything, and a season for every activity under heaven" (Ecclesiastes 3:1). We can better understand God's timing when we understand the seasons of our lives and identify which we are in.

WINTER. Cold weather and hard ground make things appear dead and unfruitful, but winter can be a very productive time. It's a time to clear out the deadwood, debris, and stones that will hinder future growth; to mend fences and repair broken machinery; to plan and prepare for the growing seasons.

Arrange your schedule and set goals. Research the resources you need, such as a support team, organizations and programs, and counselors. Use winter to prepare.

SPRING. It's a time of new beginnings and fresh hope. You plow the soil, add fertilizer and supplements, plant seeds, and irrigate. You care for the fragile shoots that appear, keeping the garden free of destructive pests.

In the spring of your life, you implement the plans you made in the winter. See a counselor, enter a program, or join a group.

SUMMER. In summer the fields are lush with healthy plants. It's a season for maintenance and protection of what you began in the spring. Don't be lulled into inactivity because good things are happening. Stay with the program; keep working at what God has given you to do.

FALL. At harvesttime you reap what you have sown. You experience and enjoy the benefits of your work.

In the fall of personal growth, you see victory in your battle with depression. It's a time of celebration and gratitude. It's a time to give back to

God and others something of what you have received.

We would all rather skip the work of winter, spring, and summer and enjoy the harvest of fall all the time. But the only way to reap a bountiful harvest is to make good use of your time in each season.

Getting to

know God and

loving him

with everything you are

is a lifelong journey.

Love God with All You Are

God loves you unconditionally, and even when you don't know how to overcome your depression, he has a way for you to do it. Following his way is a matter of love on your part. Our eighth principle for following God's way is to *love him passionately with every area of your life.*

Jesus said, "Love the Lord your God with all your heart and with all your soul and with all your mind. This is the first and greatest commandment" (Matthew 22:37–38). Loving God is the greatest

> Immerse yourself in God's love, and you will find his way to victory.

commandment because it encompasses all the others. If we love God, connect to him, and do what honors him, we will find that we are also doing what is best for us. Immerse yourself in his love, and you will find his way to victory.

Here are a few facets of your life where love for God must take the lead.

VALUES. Our values determine what is important to us. Loving God means what is important to him should be important to you.

PASSIONS. These deep urges and drives make us feel alive. Let your love for God fuel your passions.

EMOTIONS. No matter how you feel in your situation—afraid, anxious, sad, or angry—ask God to reach inside you with his love so that you will be able to feel your feelings in ways that help you grow and move on.

TALENTS. Love God with all your strengths, skills, and abilities. As you do, God will use you to make a way for others.

Think of the dearest, closest, most loving relationship in your life. What characterizes this relationship? You are probably very open and vulnerable with each other. You know each other's secrets, fears, and desires. You take risks with each other. You need and depend on each other. And this relationship makes you feel alive.

Our best human relationships are only a frail picture of the loving, intimate relationship you can enjoy with God. Learning to love him with everything you are is a lifelong journey. And the more of yourself you open up to him, the more God is able to help you through your depression.

Loving God is saying to him, "Even when I don't know how to overcome my problem, I want you to do whatever you need to do in my life." This gives him access to every part of you that needs his love, grace, and support.

You may feel connected to God in your head, theologically, but not your heart, emotionally. Or the converse may be true. Either way, begin to bring those aspects of your soul and life to his grace so that all of you is being loved and supported by God himself.

If you ever need God's way in your life, it's when you are suffering with depression. God has the will and the resources to put your life back together again. "He heals the broken-hearted and binds up their wounds" (Psalm 147:3). However, you must bring your depression to God in order to experience his love and healing.

God is all about love, and he wants us to be all about love too. The more you make everything you are accessible to him, the more you can grow, be healed, and find his way. Be sure you are not hiding your depression from God. Love God with your heart, soul, mind, and strength, and let his love set you free.

PART II:
DISCOURAGEMENT AND DEPRESSION

I was so depressed when I didn't get the raise." "I gained ten more pounds; that was really depressing." "All this rain is making me so depressed."

Most of us have made these kinds of comments to describe a negative experience or a bad day or a disappointing event. Though we are describing events and feelings that can be deeply sad and discouraging, *we are not really describing depression.* At least, not in the true and clinical sense of the word. In the last few years, the meaning of depression has changed and broadened in popular terminology to include ideas and feelings that differ significantly from what depression really is.

Those who truly understand the meaning of *depression* use the term somewhat sparingly. It is one of the most painful experiences a person can undergo. There are, however, varying degrees of severity in depression. If you are depressed, you may feel:

- utterly alone and utterly isolated, inside and outside of yourself;
- a deep self-hatred that constantly attacks your soul with condemnation and criticism;
- nonexistent, not really alive and real, numb and detached from life;
- lethargic and soul-weary, as if trying to swim in mud;
- as if you were trapped in a "black hole."

Some people who have experienced very severe depression say it is the closest thing they can imagine to being in hell.

People also respond differently to those who are depressed, and most of us hope that we will never be in that place emotionally. Some people feel confused because they can see no reason for the depressed person's feelings. They may become frustrated and angry because it can look like the depressed person isn't doing the things he or she needs to do to get better. Other people have compassion, perhaps because they have experienced the listlessness of depression themselves or because they love someone who has. They can hang on to hope when the depressed person has none, offering support through their care and prayers. Depression leaves no one unmarked or unmoved at some level.

Depression also has a life of its own, so to speak. It occurs independent of your circumstances, which is counter to what many believe. This fact is what distinguishes true depression from the feelings of discouragement or sadness that can accompany a negative event or experience. When you are feeling down or blue, your feelings can often be "cured" by changing your environment or setting, or resolving a problem or issue. For example, if you have a row with your husband or wife, you may feel distant and lonely, but usually those feelings go away after you reconcile, often leaving you feeling more alive inside and connected to each other than before. Or if you are stressed out and discouraged about your job, you may take a weekend off to go play somewhere and come back refreshed and invigorated. Many churches conduct weekend retreats for their members with this idea in mind, and they are very effective.

True depression, however, doesn't go away so easily. Teresa is a young wife and mother of two. She is healthy, intelligent, and pretty. Her husband is successful in his work; he is loving, attentive, and spends much time with Teresa and the children. She is a Christian who attends church regularly and often teaches a class of six-year-olds. She and her family live in a nice home and have no financial problems. All outward indicators would say that Teresa should never be depressed, but she fights it all the time. And her case is not unusual.

Being depressed is similar to having a bacterial infection—all the aspirin in the world will not make it go away. When you are truly depressed, though reconciled relationships and relaxing environments can help bring some relief, they don't remove the symptoms. You then become a depressed person with reconciled relationships in a relaxing environment. It is as if depressed people have a filter in their brains that interprets any words or experiences through the depression, so that they become distorted. For example, if you are depressed, a friend might tell you, "I care about what happens to you," yet you won't be able to feel any warmth or comfort from your friend's words. Instead you will likely respond with something like, "That's because you don't know me," or "I hear you, but I don't feel it."

Many people in the church do not understand this distorting filter of depression, and thus they try to help the depressed person by talking about the love of God, the hope of his provision, and all the good things he has in store for us. The depressed person will try to "take it in" and experience these truths, but it just won't happen. The filter blocks their effect. Often, in trying to bless the depressed person by reminding him or her of these promises, well-meaning people will unknowingly sever the truth of God's Word from the experience of being present with a person who cares. Depressed people need both God's truth and his love, in the form of his Spirit and his people. It takes more than the words by themselves.

This was the case with William, a pastor who had struggled with depression most of his life. For years he was able to keep his feelings of self-condemnation and loneliness at bay by occasionally seeing a counselor until he felt a little better, but he never truly resolved the issue. When he was in his early forties, however, William took a job on the pastoral staff of a large church. Within a few months he started to lose weight and couldn't sleep more than two or three hours a night. He spiraled downward, becoming more and more listless and lethargic until it impaired his ability to do his job at the church. After about six months of this, the church had to let him go, but they did so with the promise to keep him on the payroll so that he could get the help he needed. They wanted him to see a counselor and to determine whether the cause of his condition was emotional, biological, or both.

William did seek professional help. When he told his counselor that he had lost any hope of ever feeling any differently, the counselor asked him how this felt. William told him, "I don't really feel anything. I know I should feel badly about all this, but I don't. Not really." Part of the reason that he'd lost hope was his inability to feel God's love for him—or anyone else's for that matter. He knew with his mind that God loved him—after all, he'd gone to seminary—but he'd never really believed it in his heart. William's depression was severe, and it took a long period of counseling and being on medication before he began to experience good results and the hope that God was working with him in dealing with depression.

William's depression was obvious to everyone. It was impossible to be around him and not know that something was desperately wrong, but many times this isn't the case. You can be depressed and not even realize it because you don't feel sad or down or encounter hopeless feelings. However, it will show up in other ways. You may be having relationship difficulties or work difficulties, or you may be self-medicating through substances, sex, or food, which anesthetize you from the experience of depression. Your involvement in activities that are normally productive and healthy, such as work, hobbies, sports, art, or even ministry tasks, may be so intense that these prevent you from feeling sad or lonely.

Yet if you have a hidden depression, most of the time it will ultimately emerge. It will begin "leaking" out through the behaviors that cover it; or you will become aware that you are not doing these things out of freedom but out of fear or compulsion, and that you don't find true joy or satisfaction in them. You also may become aware of being depressed when you find someone who truly loves and cares for you. The other person's love and vulnerability may help to melt the inaccessible parts of you inside—parts that you were able to hide or keep closed until a relationship drew them out in the open and exposed them.

HOLDING ON TO GOD

When you face depression and don't know what to do or where to turn, God can make a way for you to overcome it—even severe and debilitating depression like William's. God is no stranger to depression; he understands it, and his nature is such that the darker the despair, the more his love and light grow. He heals most where we are injured the most: "You, O LORD, keep my lamp burning; my God turns my darkness into light" (Psalm 18:28).

If you are depressed, you need to know that you are not alone. Research indicates that a significant percentage of people will become depressed at some point in their lives. Even such famous figures as Abraham Lincoln and Winston Churchill gave indications of depression in their writings. The apostle Paul identified with depression in his own sufferings: "But God, who comforts the depressed, comforted us by the coming of Titus" (2 Corinthians 7:6 NASB). Jesus described his experience in the Garden of Gethsemane in similar terms: "Then he said to them, 'My soul is overwhelmed with sorrow to the point of death. Stay here and keep watch with me'" (Matthew 26:38).

The suffering of Jesus also helps clarify some misunderstandings about the causes of depression. Some people believe that depression is a sign of some spiritual, moral, or ethical failure or lapse—the result of the internal conflict that comes when we are bad or miss the mark. It is true that we do experience internal conflict when we are not true to being the person God intended us to be. When we stray off God's path, he gives us signals to help correct us: "When I kept silent, my bones wasted away through my groaning all day long" (Psalm 32:3). At the same time, however, it is simply not true that sin causes all depression, just as it is not true that sin causes all the pain we endure. Many bad things happen to everyone—things that they have no control over and are not their fault. Suffering and depression can have causes that have nothing to do with any moral or spiritual lapse on the part of the victim.

Some years ago I (John) went through depression. It was quite painful and disruptive for me, and it did not go away quickly. I was under a lot of stress at the time, and I began to withdraw from others. I lost some focus in my work, and I began having the negative and hopeless thoughts that accompany depression. I can remember being drawn to cloudy and rainy days. I felt that the weather and sky reflected my own internal darkness and sadness, and it served to comfort me somewhat. Even so, it was a period for me that many have called the "dark night of the soul."

It helped that I understood depression at a clinical level, because I was able to recognize the signs for what they were, and I knew the next step to take. I entered counseling and learned that much of my depression had to do with a lifelong tendency to disconnect from my own heart and not pay attention to my own needs for relation- ship. I often placed task diligence over emotional dependency. I substituted hard work for vital relationships, which left a hole in my life. This information was very valuable to me, and it enabled me to make changes that diminished my depression.

The true resolution of my depression ultimately came from God and the path that he designed for me to follow. I can remember reading and praying through verses about God's comfort for the depressed person—holding on to him, and hoping that the process he designed would end it. I found a support system of loving, honest, and safe people who I began to let inside. I learned to open up and be vulnerable to the love of God and others, as the Bible teaches (Psalm 119:76; Ecclesiastes 4:9–12; 2 Corinthians 6:11–13; Ephesians 3:17–19); and, in time, God proved faithful to his nature and his way. I am grateful to God, his realities, and the people he placed in my life to get me through it.

As clinical psychologists, we have dealt with many, many individuals who were depressed or discouraged, at all levels of severity. As in my case, some people suffering from depression can maintain good relationships, work successfully, and continue the basic tasks of life while going through the healing process. Those on the other end of the severity continuum, like William, need external structures that are more intensive—even to the point of hospitalization if the person is suicidal.

Because of all the research that has been conducted on depression, we know a lot about it. The solutions and treatments are effective not only for the short term but also in the long run. The two of us strongly believe that many, many depressions can be resolved. Even people who struggle with a chemical component to their depression can make great progress with the medication technology available today. We do not follow the notion that all victims of depression must simply learn to cope with it or resign themselves to accepting it is a part of them forever. We do not believe that depression is something they must live with and manage and that is as good as it gets. We have seen God, his resources, and his answers provide—in the process of repair—healing from depression when people have entered and stayed on his path of growth.

We have noticed, however, that those who struggle with depression fall into two categories. They tend either to avoid dealing with it, or they face it, deal with the pain, and bring it to God in the way that he prescribes. Those who try to deny it, rise above it, or use willpower to make it go away tend to suffer more in the long run. Those who put their faith and trust in God end up in a much better place. We have seen this time and again. That is why we want you to have the information needed to apply God's healing to depression.

OUT OF LIFE

According to psychological and psychiatric researchers, depression can be identified by these symptoms:

- A depressed mood

- Changes in appetite

- Changes in sleep patterns

- Fatigue

- Self-image distortions

- Problems in concentration

- Hopeless feelings

When you experience even some of these symptoms over a period of time, you are depressed.

In addition to the emotional component, depression often has a medical component. During depression the brain chemistry is altered, and medication may be required to bring about the right balance of chemicals so that the person's brain can function correctly. When the brain needs corrective medication, it signals this need by the presence of what are called vegetative symptoms—that is, symptoms that affect a person's ability to function, live, and carry out life's responsibilities. Problems with sleep, appetite, and fatigue are examples of these sorts of symptoms.

When these are in play, no amount of talking or support will resolve the chemical issue. In computer terms, it is not just a software issue now; it is also a hardware issue. The brain itself is not working as it should. Depression that has a medical component must be treated with medication. So if you struggle with a severe depression, we encourage you to consult with a psychiatrist in order to look at the possibility of medications that can help alleviate your symptoms while you are addressing the emotional and relational aspects of your healing.

At its heart, depression is a spiritual, emotional, and personal condition. That condition is best described as being *cut off from life*. Some aspect of the person's heart and soul is out of order, disengaged and disconnected from God and others. It is as if some vital part of you is lost and frozen in time, and it is inaccessible for love, relationship, grace, or the truth.

> God did not intend
> that any part of us
> be in the dark and
> out of relationship.

God did not design or create us to be disconnected from himself or the life he wanted us to have. His intent from the beginning has always been that we should experience total love and joy. In his deepest essence, God is connected to and is all about love. As the Bible simply puts it, "God is love" (1 John 4:16). We are created in his image—God intended that we be connected in love to him and to others. This connection was meant to extend to every part of our being. We are to be known and loved in our wants, needs, desires, loves, hates, sins, passions, and failures. God did not intend for any part of us to be in the dark and out of relationship.

However, the reality of life is that, for various reasons, we do get hurt or wounded inside. When that happens, we often withdraw an injured part of ourselves without even being aware that we are doing it. This withdrawal protects the injured part, but it also prevents the injured part from receiving the love and help it needs to heal. It's as if you tore a shoulder muscle while lifting a heavy item the wrong way, and then treated it by "favoring" that shoulder and not using it for a while. Yet lack of use alone is not enough to restore your muscle. To heal properly it needs exercise, massage, and physical therapy.

God designed and created you to love him with every fiber of yourself, including your heart, soul, mind, and strength. He also designed you with many complex and interrelated aspects to yourself. You have many parts to your soul and personality. And any one of these parts of your soul can get "out of life," as we will call it. That part of you has been withdrawn, as we explained above, because it has been hurt or made vulnerable. And like a torn muscle, it is not exercised and thus it loses its ability to maintain its vital function, and it's as if it were dead.

Perhaps you have no ability to grieve and let go of loves you have lost; that ability is then out of life. It's not working; it's dead. Or maybe you are unable to make emotional connections with others in the first place. If so, you may feel as if you are not part of life, or that you are almost like a ghost, seeing other people's warmth, love, and compassion for each other, but not being a part of it. You may feel as if you are looking at the real world of love and relationships through a window, but that you are unable to go into the room where it is occurring. The part of you that functions in that room is not working. It seems dead. You may never have had the ability to possess and own your own feelings and emotions; in this case, your feelings exist out of life. Or perhaps you have never been able to be separate and clear about what you will allow and tolerate and what you will refuse; thus, you may burn out and become depressed. When any of these things happen, these parts of your soul—parts that you really need—stay wounded or undeveloped inside you.

THE SOUL'S CRY FOR HELP

God is eternal and lives in eternity, and he has also made us eternal. We do not cease to exist after we have died. Similarly, the parts of us with which we have lost contact become buried and may seem dead, but they do not really die. They remain in a stuck and wounded state, deep inside us, waiting to be revived from the outside by life and light. Yet when we do not have access to all of ourselves, and when those parts of us that are stuck inside are not loved and not in the process of healing and growth, then life does not work well for us. We are missing important assets and attributes we need in order to live in an emotionally healthy way. We are handicapped in our choices, in our ability to function at high levels, and in our ability to be deeply connected to others. These wounded or hidden parts of ourselves want to come out and deal with the challenges they are meant to deal with, and it takes a great deal of energy to keep them underground, although we may not be aware that we are even doing it. Thus, handicapped and spiritually exhausted, we become depressed.

Depression is truly the soul's cry for help, and in this sense it is a blessing. Depression is an unmistakable signal that something is wrong inside that needs to be explored and understood, and it needs to have God's healing resources brought to bear upon it. In a way that few conditions do, depression brings us to our knees—to the end of ourselves—so that we will seek God's answers and ways. Many people who we have treated for depression have told us that they were grateful that God allowed the condition, terrible as it was, for it caused them to look for his answers in a way that they had not been open to or aware of before: "It was good for me to be afflicted so that I might learn your decrees" (Psalm 119:71).

What, then, are the ways that God provides for you to deal successfully with depression?

CONNECTING THE DISCONNECTED

If, instead of depression, you had a stomach ulcer, what is the first thing you would do? You'd probably go see a specialist who would examine, diagnose, and treat you. The worst thing you could do would be to avoid talking to anyone about it and hope it went away, for of course it would not go away.

The same is true with depression. No matter what is causing or driving your depression, in order for the depression to lead you to life, you need relationship. Your soul needs to experience the depth and healing of love and grace. No one gets well on his or her own. Anyone struggling with depression will need to be connected, both to God and to people. The best place to be in any situation is in relationship. Relationship is not a luxury, it is a necessity. We are created as relational beings, and our well-being depends on relationships. And this is particularly true for you if you are depressed.

As we said earlier, a lack of connection and relationship helps give rise to the depression. The nature of depression requires that you be open and vulnerable to other safe people. The presence and application of relationship will help to undo your depression, because it will draw out the broken part of your soul and enable it to receive what it has been lacking.

As you likely recognize, this can be difficult. People who care about you and love you can surround you, and yet the isolated parts of your soul may remain untouched because you can't open up and receive the healing of their love for you. It will take time for you to recognize and reach the part of your soul that you have kept from others. Initially, you may not be able to "reach out and touch someone" with the broken part of yourself, because it may simply be too inaccessible, too hurt, or too undeveloped.

I (John) have a friend, Dawn, whose depression had a lot to do with her inability to let others inside her heart. When she became a part of a therapy group to heal the depression, she could not make herself feel close to or trusting of the people in the group. In fact, she could not trust God or anyone with her heart. However, Dawn did do what she was able to do: she managed to trust God and his process enough to get involved in the group. She brought her inability, her fears, her lack of trust, and her emotional inaccessibility to these people, who then supported her, loved her and, over time, earned her trust.

Dawn did this by first quietly observing how the group interacted with each other. For a while she kept a safe distance. Then, as she noted that the members did not condemn each other

(Romans 8:1) and that they were vulnerable with each other, she began taking risks with them. She talked about her fears of opening up and being hurt, abandoned, or attacked. As the members of the group proved safe, she revealed her own experiences of having been injured by significant others, the losses she had sustained, and the things she had done to make things worse for herself.

Dawn did what people all through the centuries have done, and what you can do: reach out to God and his people with whatever you have the ability to reach out with—your need, or your commitment, or your pain, or your awareness; that is, with whatever you are in touch with about yourself, whatever is hurting, whatever you can talk about that deals with what is real in your life. God takes us in whatever state we are in, and wherever we cannot provide, he takes up the slack and goes the extra mile.

The Bible tells a story about a father of a boy who was possessed by a demon. The father took his son to Jesus, who talked to him about the importance of belief in Christ himself: "Immediately the boy's father exclaimed, 'I do believe; help me overcome my unbelief!'" (Mark 9:24). We can identify with the father's reaching out with all the belief he had, yet knowing that what he had was not enough. At that point, he humbly asked Jesus for the rest of the belief he did not possess.

All you have to do—and we admit that this can be a lot—is reach out for relationship and connection with God and others and be committed to the process of healing, to God's path for you out of depression. You can bring yourself to relationship, even in a depressed state. The best you may be able to do is to reach out to a group, a pastor, or a counselor who can give you some relational structure and tell them, "I have an aloneness inside. As I am now, I can't let you inside where it is. But I want to be as vulnerable and honest as I can so that, in time, the disconnected parts of me can also come into the relationship." Be open with those parts of your heart that you can be open with, and allow God, his love, and his people to help the rest happen.

Remember that relationship, as God has designed it, is most of what life really is. Allow relationship to fill, guide, and comfort you. That is a large part of what begins to heal and resolve depression.

As you seek connection with God and others, you should also begin exploring the cause of your depression.

REDEEMING WHAT IS LOST OR BROKEN

As we have already explained, depression can have more than one cause. Because of that, steer away from such simplistic explanations as "It is always poor self-image," or "It is always anger turned inward," or "It is always genetic and bio-logical." Humans are more complex creatures than that, and depressed people need help to explore the origins of their depression from those who understand these matters: "The purposes of a man's heart are deep waters, but a man of understanding draws them out" (Proverbs 20:5).

As you ask God to help you identify the cause of your depression, remember that he always redeems his people who have lost their way or have lost some part of themselves. God is a redemptive God. This is why he is called "my Rock and my Redeemer" (Psalm 19:14), for that is who he is and what he does. He seeks out the lost, repairs them, and helps them re-enter life to the fullest.

Here is a brief list of some of the things that can cause depression. As you go over it, see if any of these causes resonate with you. Ask those who know you if any of them make sense for your condition. And ask God to open windows inside you to help you find what is true about you:

INABILITY TO GRIEVE LOSSES. This is a very common cause of depression. When you do not have the capacity to experience your sadness over your losses in life and let go of those things you have lost, the "frozen losses" keep you stuck. That is why, when people become safe enough to feel sad about who or what they no longer have in their lives, they go through a period of grief and then the depression resolves. That is why depression and grief are so different and should not be confused with each other. Actually, grief, which may seem like depression while you are in it, is the cure for many kinds of depression.

LACK OF ABILITY TO NEED AND DEPEND ON OTHERS EMOTIONALLY. Some people have been disconnected from love and comfort all their lives. Their inner world is an empty, isolated place where they cannot reach out to anyone for their needs.

PROBLEMS IN RESPONSIBILITY AND FREEDOM. There are times when a person has trouble taking ownership and control of his or her life, or does not feel free to choose what is right for him or her.

BURNOUT. For some reason, some people give to others beyond their resources, and even have difficulty receiving what they need in order to continue.

PERFECTIONISM. The perfectionist will often become depressed as the reality of his or her failings and weaknesses becomes too much to bear.

FEELINGS OF SELF-CONDEMNATION. This is an individual's suffering from an unbiblical, overcritical, and harsh conscience that attacks him or her even when he or she has done no wrong.

UNRESOLVED TRAUMA. When a person has experienced a catastrophic event or injury that is not processed, confessed, grieved, and worked through, it can contribute to depression.

MEDICAL CAUSES. Some depressions are caused or influenced by a problem in brain chemistry, as we mentioned previously, or by other medical conditions that produce depression. Make sure you have adequate medical input here. A complete physical by a general practitioner and a psychiatric workup by a psychiatrist might be in order.

As you seek to discover which part of you has been lost, think of it as a part of you that you need in order to function well in life. Look at the preceding list. Why do you need the ability to grieve? Why is it important that you experience need? Why is it necessary to be clear about your responsibilities? Learn the value and purpose of the lost part of yourself. It will help you to see how much you need it.

Then, as that part emerges in the context of warm, safe, and loving relationships, begin allowing yourself to feel the feelings that go along with it. Experience the hurt that made that part disappear in the first place. Keep exposing it to the nurture and care of relationships. As it strengthens, take small risks with it. Learn to use it again in your life. Let it take its place in your world. Over time, allow that part of you to mature, grow up, and simply be a part of you that you again own, utilize, and experience.

Clearly, doing this will require a mentor. You will need someone who has good experience with depression, as there is a great deal to know about it. Find such a person and follow his or her guidance, and God's, as the part of you that is lost becomes found.

Depression can be debilitating and frightening. However, God is right there with you in the black hole, as he fills it up with love and light and provides a way out, back into his world. Trust him for that.

PART III:
BEGIN YOUR JOURNEY TODAY

Y ou are near the end of this book, but you are only at the beginning of the journey God is making for you to overcome your depression. You may have come to this book not knowing what to do in the face of your despair. We have shown you that God has a way for you, and we have tried to prepare you to walk in that way. In the earlier sections we filled your pack with supplies and put a map in your hands. Now it's time for you to hit the trail. As you do, we leave you with three final words of advice.

WALK IN GRACE. Your first step on the journey, and every subsequent step, is a step into God's grace. Simply put, grace is God's *unmerited favor*. This means that God is on your side. He wants you to resolve your depression and is committed to work in you, with you, and through you to accomplish it. God loves you completely, and he's going with you every step of the way. He will be your biggest cheerleader.

STEP OUT IN FAITH. You need two strong legs to complete a strenuous hike—right, left, right, left, one after the other. Similarly, in your journey with God, faith is a two-step process. It is both an *attitude* and an *action*. You believe God loves you, but you need to love him in return. You know God will speak to you, but you need to listen attentively. You have faith that God will guide you and protect you, but you need to follow him and submit to his care. Whenever you take a step of *faith* in God, follow it with a step of *action*.

STAY ON THE TRAIL. Now that your feet are moving, let's take one last look at the trail ahead. This is the way God has made for you. It may be strenuous in trying times, but it is full of discovery and wonder. And the destination is well worth the effort. Here are ten key reminders that will help keep you on the trail and moving forward.

1. Set goals. What do you want God to do for you? Decide now, and be specific. Make your goal as clear and concise as possible so you can envision it, pray about it, and decide on a specific strategy to reach it.

2. Record progress. Write down your goal and put it where you can see it often—on the fridge, on the bathroom mirror, in your daily planner or journal, beside your desk or workstation, or elsewhere. Also write down each significant insight as you step toward your goal.

3. Gather resources. Start looking for the people, programs, and organizations who can assist you on the journey. The better your resources, the faster you should reach your goal.

4. Acquire information. Educate yourself on the type of depression you are facing. Is it truly depression or a temporary discouragement? If it is depression, do the symptoms point toward medical or psychological treatment? Studies show that those who are more knowledgeable about their conditions do better in treatment. They ask insightful questions and sometimes notice things a doctor might miss. As much as possible, become an expert in the area of your depression.

5. Identify tasks. Give yourself specific assignments: thought patterns to adopt, actions to perform, emotions to express, habits to form, and so forth. Break your tasks into manageable portions and take them one by one.

6. Evaluate progress. Review your progress at defined intervals. Are you making headway? If not, why not? Put your evaluation in writing for future reference, and make any necessary adjustments to your plan.

7. Explore preferences. Tailor your plan and tasks to your individual preferences. You will likely have many choices on your journey: counselors, programs, classes, and organizations.

8. Remain flexible. Don't cast your plan in stone. It exists to serve your growth. If your plan is not getting results over a reasonable period of time, rethink it and make changes. And even when your plan is working, stay alert to ways you can improve it.

9. Pray continually. When you pray, you're not talking to the wall or to yourself. You are talking to God, and he hears you and responds. Prayer is a genuine and powerful ally on your journey. It's not your prayers that have the power; it's God on the other end of the line who has the power to do what you cannot do. Don't take one step without talking to God about it.

10. Pace yourself. This is a journey, not a race. Few changes happen overnight, no matter how hard you work or pray. Give God time to work, and be thankful for the little changes you see.

We are pleased that you are so interested in following God's way to freedom from depression. We pray that the God in whom we live, move, and exist will guide and sustain you on the journey, both today and forever. God bless you!

—Henry Cloud, Ph.D.
—John Townsend, Ph.D.
Los Angeles, California

EMBARK ON A
LIFE-CHANGING JOURNEY
OF PERSONAL AND SPIRITUAL GROWTH

DR. HENRY CLOUD   **DR. JOHN TOWNSEND**

Dr. Henry Cloud and Dr. John Townsend have been bringing hope and healing to millions for over two decades. They have helped people everywhere discover solutions to life's most difficult personal and relational challenges. Their material provides solid, practical answers and offers guidance in the areas of *parenting, singles issues, personal growth,* and *leadership.*

Bring either Dr. Cloud or Dr. Townsend to your church or organization. They are available for:

- Seminars on a wide variety of topics
- Training for small group leaders
- Conferences
- Educational events
- Consulting with your organization

Other opportunities to experience Dr. Cloud and Dr. Townsend:

- Ultimate Leadership workshops—held in Southern California throughout the year
- Small group curriculum
- Seminars via Satellite
- Solutions Audio Club—Solutions is a weekly recorded presentation

For other resources, and for dates of seminars and workshops
by Dr. Cloud and Dr. Townsend, visit:
www.cloudtownsend.com

For other information **Call (800) 676-HOPE (4673)**

Or write to:
Cloud-Townsend Resources
3176 Pullman Street, Suite 105
Costa Mesa, CA